THE DUTIES OF PARENTS

JOHN CHARLES RYLE

CONTENTS

John Charles Ryle	1
Introduction	2
1. Train Your Child Rightly	6
2. Tenderness, Affection and Patience	8
3. Much Depends on You	12
4. Consider the Soul of Your Child	16
5. A Knowledge of the Bible	19
6. A Habit of Prayer	23
7. Diligence in the Public Means of Grace	28
8. A Habit of Faith	32
9. A Habit of Obedience	36
10. Always Speaking the Truth	40
11. Redeeming the Time	43
12. Fear Over-Indulgence	47
13. How God Trains His Children	52
14. The Influence of Your Example	57
15. The Power of Sin	60
16. The Promises of Scripture	62
17. Continual Prayer for Blessing	65

JOHN CHARLES RYLE

First Anglican Bishop Of Liverpool
CHURCH OF ENGLAND
1816—1900

INTRODUCTION

> "Train up a child in the way he should go; and when he is old, he will not depart from it."
>
> — PROV 22:6.

I suppose that most professing Christians are acquainted with the text at the head of this page. The sound of it is probably familiar to your ears, like an old tune. It is likely you have heard it, or read it, talked of it, or quoted it, many a time. Is it not so?

But, after all, how little is the substance of this text regarded! The doctrine it contains appears scarcely known, the duty it puts before us seems fearfully seldom practised. Reader, do I not speak the truth? It cannot be said that the subject is a new one. The world is old, and we have the experience of nearly six thousand years to help us. We live in days when there is a mighty zeal for education in every quarter. We hear of new schools rising on all sides. We are told of new systems, and new books for the young, of every sort and description. And still for all this, the vast majority of children are manifestly not trained in the way they should go, for when they grow up to man's estate, they do not walk with God. Now how shall we account for this state of things? The plain truth is, the Lord's commandment in our text is not regarded; and therefore the Lord's promise in our text is not fulfilled.

Reader, these things may well give rise to great searchings of heart. Suffer then a word of exhortation from a minister, about the right training of children. Believe me, the subject is one that should come home to every conscience, and make every one ask himself the question, "Am I in this matter doing what I can?"

It is a subject that concerns almost all. There is hardly a household that it does not touch. Parents, nurses, teachers, godfathers, godmothers, uncles, aunts, brothers, sisters, — all have an interest in it. Few can be found, I think, who might not influence some parent in the management of his family, or affect the training of some child by suggestion or advice. All of us, I suspect, can do something here, either directly or indirectly, and I wish to stir up all to bear this in remembrance.

It is a subject, too, on which all concerned are in great danger of coming short of their duty. This is preeminently a point in which men can see the faults of their neighbours more clearly than their own. They will often bring up their children in the very path which they have denounced to their friends as unsafe. They will see motes in other men's families, and overlook beams in their own. They will be quick sighted as eagles in detecting mistakes abroad, and yet blind as bats to fatal errors which are daily going on at home. They will be wise about their brother's house, but foolish about their own flesh and blood. Here, if anywhere, we have need to suspect our own judgment. This, too, you will do well to bear in mind[1].

Come now, and let me place before you a few hints about right training. God the Father, God the Son, God the Holy Ghost bless them, and make them words in season to you all. Reject them not because they are blunt and simple; despise them not because they contain nothing new. Be very sure, if you would train children for heaven, they are hints that ought not to be lightly set aside.

---

1. As a minister, I cannot help remarking that there is hardly any subject about which people seem so tenacious as they are about their children. I have sometimes been perfectly astonished at the slowness of sensible Christian parents to allow that their own children are in fault, or deserve blame. There are not a few persons to whom I would far rather speak about their own sins, than tell them their children had done anything wrong.

1

TRAIN YOUR CHILD RIGHTLY

First, then, if you would train your children rightly, train them in the way they should go, and not in the way that they would.

Remember children are born with a decided bias towards evil, and therefore if you let them choose for themselves, they are certain to choose wrong. The mother cannot tell what her tender infant may grow up to be, — tall or short, weak or strong, wise or foolish he may be any of these things or not, — it is all uncertain. But one thing the mother can say with certainty: he will have a corrupt and sinful heart. It is natural to us to do wrong. "Foolishness," says Solomon, "is bound in the heart of a child" (Prov. 22:15). "A child left to himself bringeth his mother to shame" (Prov. 29:15).

Our hearts are like the earth on which we tread; let it alone, and it is sure to bear weeds. If, then, you would deal wisely with your child, you must not leave him to the guidance of his own will. Think for him, judge for him, act for him, just as you would for one weak and blind; but for pity's sake, give him not up to his own wayward tastes and inclinations. It must not be his likings and wishes that are consulted. He knows not yet what is good for his mind and soul, any more than what is good for his body. You do not let him decide what he shall eat, and what he shall drink, and how he shall be clothed. Be consistent, and deal with his mind in like manner. Train him in the way that is scriptural and right, and not in the way that he fancies.

If you cannot make up your mind to this first principle of Christian training, it is useless for you to read any further. Self-will is almost the first thing that appears in a child's mind; and it must be your first step to resist it.

2
TENDERNESS, AFFECTION AND PATIENCE

Train up your child with all tenderness, affection, and patience. I do not mean that you are to spoil him, but I do mean that you should let him see that you love him.

Love should be the silver thread that runs through all your conduct. Kindness, gentleness, long-suffering, forbearance, patience, sympathy, a willingness to enter into childish troubles, a readiness to take part in childish joys, — these are the cords by which a child may be led most easily, — these are the clues you must follow if you would find the way to his heart. Few are to be found, even among grown-up people, who are not more easy to draw than to drive. There is that in all our minds which rises in arms against compulsion; we set up our backs and stiffen our necks at the very idea of a forced obedience. We are like young horses in the hand of a breaker: handle them kindly, and make much of them, and by and by you may guide them with thread; use them roughly and violently, and it will be many a month before you get the mastery of them at all.

Now children's minds are cast in much the same mould as our own. Sternness and severity of manner chill them and throw them back. It shuts up their hearts, and you will weary yourself to find the door. But let them only see that you have an affectionate feeling towards them, — that you are really desirous to make them happy, and do them good, — that if you punish them, it is intended for their profit, and that, like the pelican, you would give your heart's blood to nourish their souls; let them see this, I say, and they will soon be all your own. But they must be wooed with kindness, if their attention is ever to be won. And surely reason itself might teach us this lesson. Children are weak and tender creatures, and, as such, they need patient and considerate treatment. We must handle them delicately, like frail machines, lest by rough fingering we do more harm than good. They are like young plants, and need gentle watering, — often, but little at a time.

We must not expect all things at once. We must

remember what children are, and teach them as they are able to bear. Their minds are like a lump of metal — not to be forged and made useful at once, but only by a succession of little blows. Their understandings are like narrow-necked vessels: we must pour in the wine of knowledge gradually, or much of it will be spilled and lost. "Line upon line, and precept upon precept, here a little and there a little," must be our rule. The whetstone does its work slowly, but frequent rubbing will bring the scythe to a fine edge. Truly there is need of patience in training a child, but without it nothing can be done.

Nothing will compensate for the absence of this tenderness and love. A minister may speak the truth as it is in Jesus, clearly, forcibly, unanswerably; but if he does not speak it in love, few souls will be won. Just so you must set before your children their duty, — command, threaten, punish, reason, — but if affection be wanting in your treatment, your labour will be all in vain.

Love is one grand secret of successful training. Anger and harshness may frighten, but they will not persuade the child that you are right; and if he sees you often out of temper, you will soon cease to have his respect. A father who speaks to his son as Saul did to Jonathan (1 Sam. 20:30), need not expect to retain his influence over that son's mind.

Try hard to keep up a hold on your child's affections. It is a dangerous thing to make your children afraid of you. Anything is almost better than reserve and constraint between your child and yourself; and this will come in with fear. Fear puts an end to openness of manner; — fear leads to concealment; — fear sows the seed of much hypocrisy, and leads to many a lie. There is a mine of truth in the Apostle's words to the Colossians: "Fathers, provoke not your children to anger, lest they be discouraged" (Col. 3:21). Let not the advice it contains be overlooked.

3

MUCH DEPENDS ON YOU

Train your children with an abiding persuasion on your mind that much depends upon you.

Grace is the strongest of all principles. See what a revolution grace effects when it comes into the heart of an old sinner, — how it overturns the strongholds of Satan, — how it casts down mountains, fills up valleys, — makes crooked things straight, — and new creates the whole man. Truly nothing is impossible to grace. Nature, too, is very strong. See how it struggles against the things of the kingdom of God, — how it fights against every attempt to be more holy, — how it keeps up an unceasing warfare within us to the last hour of life. Nature indeed is strong.

But after nature and grace, undoubtedly, there is nothing more powerful than education. Early habits (if I may so speak) are everything with us, under God. We are made what we are by training. Our character takes the form of that mould into which our first years are cast[1].

We depend, in a vast measure, on those who bring us up. We get from them a colour, a taste, a bias which cling to us more or less all our lives. We catch the language of our nurses and mothers, and learn to speak it almost insensibly, and unquestionably we catch something of their manners, ways, and mind at the same time. Time only will show, I suspect, how much we all owe to early impressions, and how many things in us may be traced up to seeds sown in the days of our very infancy, by those who were about us. A very learned Englishman, Mr. Locke, has gone so far as to say: "That of all the men we meet with, nine parts out of ten are what they are, good or bad, useful or not, according to their education."

And all this is one of God's merciful arrangements. He gives your children a mind that will receive impressions like moist clay. He gives them a disposition at the starting-point of life to believe what you tell them, and to take for granted what you advise them, and to trust your word rather than a stranger's.

He gives you, in short, a golden opportunity of doing them good. See that the opportunity be not neglected, and thrown away. Once let slip, it is gone for ever. Beware of that miserable delusion into which some have fallen, — that parents can do nothing for their children, that you must leave them alone, wait for grace, and sit still. These persons have wishes for their children in Balaam's fashion, — they would like them to die the death of the righteous man, but they do nothing to make them live his life. They desire much, and have nothing. And the devil rejoices to see such reasoning, just as he always does over anything which seems to excuse indolence, or to encourage neglect of means.

I know that you cannot convert your child. I know well that they who are born again are born, not of the will of man, but of God. But I know also that God says expressly, "Train up a child in the way he should go," and that He never laid a command on man which He would not give man grace to perform. And I know, too, that our duty is not to stand still and dispute, but to go forward and obey. It is just in the going forward that God will meet us. The path of obedience is the way in which He gives the blessing. We have only to do as the servants were commanded at the marriage feast in Cana, to fill the water-pots with water, and we may safely leave it to the Lord to turn that water into wine.

---

1. "He has seen but little of life who does not discern everywhere the effect of education on men's opinions and habits of thinking. The children bring out of the nursery that which displays itself throughout their lives." — Cecil.

4

CONSIDER THE SOUL OF YOUR
CHILD

Train with this thought continually before your eyes — that the soul of your child is the first thing to be considered.

Precious, no doubt, are these little ones in your eyes; but if you love them, think often of their souls. No interest should weigh with you so much as their eternal interests. No part of them should be so dear to you as that part which will never die. The world, with all its glory, shall pass away; the hills shall melt; the heavens shall be wrapped together as a scroll; the sun shall cease to shine. But the spirit which dwells in those little creatures, whom you love so well, shall outlive them all, and whether in happiness or misery (to speak as a man) will depend on you.

This is the thought that should be uppermost on your mind in all you do for your children. In every step you take about them, in every plan, and scheme, and arrangement that concerns them, do not leave out that mighty question, "How will this affect their souls?"

Soul love is the soul of all love. To pet and pamper and indulge your child, as if this world was all he had to look to, and this life the only season for happiness — to do this is not true love, but cruelty. It is treating him like some beast of the earth, which has but one world to look to, and nothing after death. It is hiding from him that grand truth, which he ought to be made to learn from his very infancy, — that the chief end of his life is the salvation of his soul.

A true Christian must be no slave to fashion, if he would train his child for heaven. He must not be content to do things merely because they are the custom of the world; to teach them and instruct them in certain ways, merely because it is usual; to allow them to read books of a questionable sort, merely because everybody else reads them; to let them form habits of a doubtful tendency, merely because they are the habits of the day. He must train with an eye to his children's souls. He must not be ashamed to hear his training called singular and strange. What if it is? The time is short, — the fashion of this world passeth away. He that has trained his children for heaven, rather than for earth, — for God, rather than for man, — he is the parent that will be called wise at last.

5
A KNOWLEDGE OF THE BIBLE

Train your child to a knowledge of the Bible.

You cannot make your children love the Bible, I allow. None but the Holy Ghost can give us a heart to delight in the Word. But you can make your children acquainted with the Bible; and be sure they cannot be acquainted with that blessed book too soon, or too well.

A thorough knowledge of the Bible is the foundation of all clear views of religion. He that is well-grounded in it will not generally be found a waverer, and carried about by every wind of new doctrine. Any system of training which does not make a knowledge of Scripture the first thing is unsafe and unsound. You have need to be careful on this point just now, for the devil is abroad, and error abounds.

Some are to be found amongst us who give the Church the honour due to Jesus Christ. Some are to be found who make the sacraments saviours and passports to eternal life. And some are to be found in like manner who honour a catechism more than the Bible, or fill the minds of their children with miserable little story-books, instead of the Scripture of truth. But if you love your children, let the simple Bible be everything in the training of their souls; and let all other books go down and take the second place. Care not so much for their being mighty in the catechism, as for their being mighty in the Scriptures. This is the training, believe me, that God will honour. The Psalmist says of Him, " Thou hast magnified Thy Word above all Thy name" (Ps. 138:2); and I think that He gives an especial blessing to all who try to magnify it among men.

See that your children read the Bible reverently. Train them to look on it, not as the word of men, but as it is in truth, the Word of God, written by the Holy Ghost Himself, — all true, all profitable, and able to make us wise unto salvation, through faith which is in Christ Jesus.

See that they read it regularly. Train them to regard it as their soul's daily food, — as a thing essential to their soul's daily health. I know well you can not make this anything more than a form; but there is no telling the amount of sin which a mere form may indirectly restrain.

See that they read it all. You need not shrink from bringing any doctrine before them. You need not fancy that the leading doctrines of Christianity are things which children cannot understand. Children understand far more of the Bible than we are apt to suppose.

Tell them of sin, its guilt, its consequences, its power, its vileness: you will find they can comprehend something of this.

Tell them of the Lord Jesus Christ, and His work for our salvation, — the atonement, the cross, the blood, the sacrifice, the intercession: you will discover there is something not beyond them in all this.

Tell them of the work of the Holy Spirit in man's heart, how He changes, and renews, and sanctifies, and purifies: you will soon see they can go along with you in some measure in this. In short, I suspect we have no idea how much a little child can take in of the length and breadth of the glorious gospel. They see far more of these things than we suppose[1].

Fill their minds with Scripture. Let the Word dwell in them richly. Give them the Bible, the whole Bible, even while they are young.

———————————————

1. As to the age when the religious instruction of a child should begin, no general rule can be laid down. The mind seems to open in some children much more quickly than in others. We seldom begin too early. There are wonderful examples on record of what a child can attain to, even at three years old.

6
A HABIT OF PRAYER

Train them to a habit of prayer.

Prayer is the very life-breath of true religion. It is one of the first evidences that a man is born again. "Behold," said the Lord of Saul, in the day he sent Ananias to him, "Behold, he prayeth" (Acts 9:11). He had begun to pray, and that was proof enough.

Prayer was the distinguishing mark of the Lord's people in the day that there began to be a separation between them and the world. "Then began men to call upon the name of the Lord" (Gen. 4:26).

Prayer is the peculiarity of all real Christians now. They pray, — for they tell God their wants, their feelings, their desires, their fears; and mean what they say. The nominal Christian may repeat prayers, and good prayers too, but he goes no further.

Prayer is the turning-point in a man's soul. Our ministry is unprofitable, and our labour is vain, till you are brought to your knees. Till then, we have no hope about you.

Prayer is one great secret of spiritual prosperity. When there is much private communion with God, your soul will grow like the grass after rain; when there is little, all will be at a standstill, you will barely keep your soul alive. Show me a growing Christian, a going forward Christian, a strong Christian, a flourishing Christian, and sure am I, he is one that speaks often with his Lord. He asks much, and he has much. He tells Jesus everything, and so he always knows how to act.

Prayer is the mightiest engine God has placed in our hands. It is the best weapon to use in every difficulty, and the surest remedy in every trouble. It is the key that unlocks the treasury of promises, and the hand that draws forth grace and help in time of need. It is the silver trumpet God commands us to sound in all our necessity, and it is the cry He has promised always to attend to, even as a loving mother to the voice of her child.

Prayer is the simplest means that man can use in

coming to God. It is within reach of all, — the sick, the aged, the infirm, the paralytic, the blind, the poor, the unlearned, — all can pray. It avails you nothing to plead want of memory, and want of learning, and want of books, and want of scholarship in this matter. So long as you have a tongue to tell your soul's state, you may and ought to pray. Those words, "Ye have not, because ye ask not" (Jas. 4:2), will be a fearful condemnation to many in the day of judgment.

Parents, if you love your children, do all that lies in your power to train them up to a habit of prayer. Show them how to begin. Tell them what to say. Encourage them to persevere. Remind them if they become careless and slack about it. Let it not be your fault, at any rate, if they never call on the name of the Lord. This, remember, is the first step in religion which a child is able to take. Long before he can read, you can teach him to kneel by his mother's side, and repeat the simple words of prayer and praise which she puts in his mouth. And as the first steps in any undertaking are always the most important, so is the manner in which your children's prayers are prayed, a point which deserves your closest attention. Few seem to know how much depends on this. You must beware lest they get into a way of saying them in a hasty, careless, and irreverent manner.

You must beware of giving up the oversight of this matter to servants and nurses, or of trusting too much to your children doing it when left to themselves. I cannot praise that mother who never looks after this most important part of her child's daily life herself. Surely if there be any habit which your own hand and eye should help in forming, it is the habit of prayer. Believe me, if you never hear your children pray yourself, you are much to blame. You are little wiser than the bird described in Job, "which leaveth her eggs in the earth, and warmeth them in the dust, and forgetteth that the foot may crush them, or that the wild beast may break them. She is hardened against her young ones, as though they were not hers: her labour is in vain without fear" (Job 39:14-16).

Prayer is, of all habits, the one which we recollect the longest. Many a grey- headed man could tell you how his mother used to make him pray in the days of his childhood. Other things have passed away from his mind perhaps. The church where he was taken to worship, the minister whom he heard preach, the companions who used to play with him, — all these, it may be, have passed from his memory, and left no mark behind. But you will often find it is far different with his first prayers. He will often be able to tell you where he knelt, and what he was taught to say, and even how his mother looked all the while. It will come up as fresh before his mind's eye as if it was but yesterday.

Reader, if you love your children, I charge you, do not let the seed-time of a prayerful habit pass away unimproved. If you train your children to anything, train them, at least, to a habit of prayer.

7
DILIGENCE IN THE PUBLIC MEANS OF GRACE

Train them to habits of diligence, and regularity about public means of grace.

Tell them of the duty and privilege of going to the house of God, and joining in the prayers of the congregation. Tell them that wherever the Lord's people are gathered together, there the Lord Jesus is present in an especial manner, and that those who absent themselves must expect, like the Apostle Thomas, to miss a blessing. Tell them of the importance of hearing the Word preached, and that it is God's ordinance for converting, sanctifying, and building up the souls of men. Tell them how the Apostle Paul enjoins us not "to forsake the assembling of ourselves together, as the manner of some is" (Heb. 10:25); but to exhort one another, to stir one another up to it, and so much the more as we see the day approaching.

I call it a sad sight in a church when nobody comes up to the Lord's table but the elderly people, and the young men and the young women all turn away. But I call it a sadder sight still when no children are to be seen in a church, excepting those who come to the Sunday School, and are obliged to attend. Let none of this guilt lie at your doors. There are many boys and girls in every parish, besides those who come to school, and you who are their parents and friends should see to it that they come with you to church.

Do not allow them to grow up with a habit of making vain excuses for not coming. Give them plainly to understand, that so long as they are under your roof it is the rule of your house for every one in health to honour the Lord's house upon the Lord's day, and that you reckon the Sabbath-breaker to be a murderer of his own soul.

See to it too, if it can be so arranged, that your children go with you to church, and sit near you when they are there. To go to church is one thing, but to behave well at church is quite another. And believe me, there is no security for good behaviour like that of having them under your own eye.

The minds of young people are easily drawn

aside, and their attention lost, and every possible means should be used to counteract this. I do not like to see them coming to church by themselves, — they often get into bad company by the way, and so learn more evil on the Lord's day than in all the rest of the week. Neither do I like to see what I call "a young people's corner" in a church. They often catch habits of inattention and irreverence there, which it takes years to unlearn, if ever they are unlearned at all. What I like to see is a whole family sitting together, old and young, side by side, — men, women, and children, serving God according to their households.

But there are some who say that it is useless to urge children to attend means of grace, because they cannot understand them.

I would not have you listen to such reasoning. I find no such doctrine in the Old Testament. When Moses goes before Pharaoh (Ex. 10:9), I observe he says, "We will go with our young and with our old, with our sons and with our daughters: for we must hold a feast unto the Lord." When Joshua read the law (Josh. 8:35), I observe, "There was not a word which Joshua read not before all the congregation of Israel, with the women and the little ones, and the strangers that were conversant among them." "Thrice in the year," says Ex. 34:23, "shall all your men-children appear before the Lord God, the God of Israel." And when I turn to the New Testament, I find children mentioned there as partaking in public acts of religion as well as in the Old. When Paul was leaving the disciples at Tyre for the last time, I find it said (Acts 21:5)," They all brought us on our way, with wives and children, till we were out of the city: and we kneeled down on the shore, and prayed."

Samuel, in the days of his childhood, appears to have ministered unto the Lord some time before he really knew Him. "Samuel did not yet know the Lord, neither was the word of the Lord yet revealed unto him" (1 Sam. 3:7). The Apostles themselves do not seem to have understood all that our Lord said at the time that it was spoken: "These things understood not His disciples at the first: but when Jesus was glorified, then remembered they that these things were written of Him" (John 12:16).

Parents, comfort your minds with these examples. Be not cast down because your children see not the full value of the means of grace now. Only train them up to a habit of regular attendance. Set it before their minds as a high, holy, and solemn duty, and believe me, the day will very likely come when they will bless you for your deed.

8

A HABIT OF FAITH

Train them to a habit of faith.

I mean by this, you should train them up to believe what you say. You should try to make them feel confidence in your judgment, and respect your opinions, as better than their own. You should accustom them to think that, when you say a thing is bad for them, it must be bad, and when you say it is good for them, it must be good; that your knowledge, in short, is better than their own, and that they may rely implicitly on your word. Teach them to feel that what they know not now, they will probably know hereafter, and to be satisfied there is a reason and a needs-be for everything you require them to do.

Who indeed can describe the blessedness of a real spirit of faith? Or rather, who can tell the misery that unbelief has brought upon the world? Unbelief made Eve eat the forbidden fruit, — she doubted the truth of God's word: "Ye shall surely die." Unbelief made the old world reject Noah's warning, and so perish in sin. Unbelief kept Israel in the wilderness, — it was the bar that kept them from entering the promised land. Unbelief made the Jews crucify the Lord of glory, — they believed not the voice of Moses and the prophets, though read to them every day. And unbelief is the reigning sin of man's heart down to this very hour, — unbelief in God's promises, — unbelief in God's threatenings, — unbelief in our own sinfulness, — unbelief in our own danger, — unbelief in everything that runs counter to the pride and worldliness of our evil hearts. Reader, you train your children to little purpose if you do not train them to a habit of implicit faith, — faith in their parents' word, confidence that what their parents say must be right.

I have heard it said by some, that you should require nothing of children which they cannot understand that you should explain and give a reason for everything you desire them to do. I warn you solemnly against such a notion. I tell you plainly, I think it an unsound and rotten principle. No doubt it is absurd to make a mystery of everything you do, and there are many things which it is well to explain to children, in order that they may see that they are reasonable and wise. But to bring them up with the idea that they must take nothing on trust, that they, with their weak and imperfect understandings, must have the "why" and the "wherefore" made clear to them at every step they take, — this is indeed a fearful mistake, and likely to have the worst effect on their minds.

Reason with your child if you are so disposed, at certain times, but never forget to keep him in mind (if you really love him) that he is but a child after all, — that he thinks as a child, he understands as a child, and therefore must not expect to know the reason of everything at once.

Set before him the example of Isaac, in the day when Abraham took him to offer him on Mount Moriah (Gen. 22). He asked his father that single question, "Where is the lamb for a burnt-offering?" and he got no answer but this, "God will provide Himself a lamb." How, or where, or whence, or in what manner, or by what means, — all this Isaac was not told; but the answer was enough. He believed that it would be well, because his father said so, and he was content. Tell your children, too, that we must all be learners in our beginnings, that there is an alphabet to be mastered in every kind of knowledge, — that the best horse in the world had need once to be broken, — that a day will come when they will see the wisdom of all your training. But in the meantime if you say a thing is right, it must be enough for them, — they must believe you, and be content.

Parents, if any point in training is important, it is this. I charge you by the affection you have to your children, use every means to train them up to a habit of faith.

9
A HABIT OF OBEDIENCE

Train them to a habit of obedience.

This is an object which it is worth any labour to attain. No habit, I suspect, has such an influence over our lives as this. Parents, determine to make your children obey you, though it may cost you much trouble, and cost them many tears. Let there be no questioning, and reasoning, and disputing, and delaying, and answering again. When you give them a command, let them see plainly that you will have it done.

Obedience is the only reality. It is faith visible, faith acting, and faith incarnate. It is the test of real discipleship among the Lord's people. "Ye are My friends if ye do whatsoever I command you" (John

15:14). It ought to be the mark of well-trained children, that they do whatsoever their parents command them. Where, in deed, is the honour which the fifth commandment enjoins, if fathers and mothers are not obeyed cheerfully, willingly, and at once?

Early obedience has all Scripture on its side. It is in Abraham's praise, not merely he will train his family, but "he will command his children, and his household after him" (Gen. 18:19). It is said of the Lord Jesus Christ Himself, that when "He was young He was subject to Mary and Joseph" (Luke 2:51).

Observe how implicitly Joseph obeyed the order of his father Jacob (Gen. 37:13). See how Isaiah speaks of it as an evil thing, when "the child shall behave himself proudly against the ancient" (Isa. 3:5). Mark how the Apostle Paul names disobedience to parents as one of the bad signs of the latter days (2 Tim. 3:2). Mark how he singles out this grace of requiring obedience as one that should adorn a Christian minister: "a bishop must be one that ruleth well his own house, having his children in subjection with all gravity." And again, "Let the deacons rule their children and their own houses well " (1 Tim. 3:4,12). And again, an elder must be one "having faithful children, children not accused of riot, or unruly" (Tit. 1:6).

Parents, do you wish to see your children happy? Take care, then, that you train them to obey when they are spoken to, — to do as they are bid. Believe me, we are not made for entire independence, — we are not fit for it. Even Christ's freemen have a yoke to wear, they "serve the Lord Christ" (Col. 3:24). Children cannot learn too soon that this is a world in which we are not all intended to rule, and that we are never in our right place until we know how to obey our betters. Teach them to obey while young, or else they will be fretting against God all their lives long, and wear themselves out with the vain idea of being independent of His control.

Reader, this hint is only too much needed. You will see many in this day who allow their children to choose and think for themselves long before they are able, and even make excuses for their disobedience, as if it were a thing not to be blamed. To my eyes, a parent always yielding, and a child always having its own way, are a most painful sight; — painful, because I see God's appointed order of things inverted and turned upside down; — painful, because I feel sure the consequence to that child's character in the end will be self-will, pride, and self-conceit. You must not wonder that men refuse to obey their Father which is in heaven, if you allow them, when children, to disobey their father who is upon earth.

Parents, if you love your children, let obedience be a motto and a watchword continually before their eyes.

10
ALWAYS SPEAKING THE TRUTH

Train them to a habit of always speaking the truth.

Truth-speaking is far less common in the world than at first sight we are disposed to think. The whole truth, and nothing but the truth, is a golden rule which many would do well to bear in mind. Lying and prevarication are old sins. The devil was the father of them, — he deceived Eve by a bold lie, and ever since the fall it is a sin against which all the children of Eve have need to be on their guard.

Only think how much falsehood and deceit there is in the world! How much exaggeration! How many additions are made to a simple story! How many things left out, if it does not serve the speaker's interest to tell them! How few there are about us of whom we can say, we put unhesitating trust in their word! Verily the ancient Persians were wise in their generation: it was a leading point with them in educating their children, that they should learn to speak the truth. What an awful proof it is of man's natural sinfulness, that it should be needful to name such a point at all!

Reader, I would have you remark how often God is spoken of in the Old Testament as the God of truth. Truth seems to be especially set before us as a leading feature in the character of Him with whom we have to do. He never swerves from the straight line. He abhors lying and hypocrisy. Try to keep this continually before your children's minds. Press upon them at all times, that less than the truth is a lie; that evasion, excuse-making, and exaggeration are all halfway houses towards what is false, and ought to be avoided. Encourage them in any circumstances to be straightforward, and, whatever it may cost them, to speak the truth.

I press this subject on your attention, not merely for the sake of your children's character in the world, — though I might dwell much on this, — I urge it rather for your own comfort and assistance in all your dealings with them. You will find it a mighty help indeed, to be able always to trust their word. It will go far to prevent that habit of concealment, which so unhappily prevails sometimes among children. Openness and straightforwardness depend much upon a parent's treatment of this matter in the days of our infancy.

11

REDEEMING THE TIME

Train them to a habit of always redeeming the time.

Idleness is the devil's best friend. It is the surest way to give him an opportunity of doing us harm. An idle mind is like an open door, and if Satan does not enter in himself by it, it is certain he will throw in something to raise bad thoughts in our souls.

No created being was ever meant to be idle. Service and work is the appointed portion of every creature of God. The angels in heaven work, — they are the Lord's ministering servants, ever doing His will. Adam, in Paradise, had work, — he was appointed to dress the garden of Eden, and to keep it.

The redeemed saints in glory will have work, "They rest not day and night singing praise and glory to Him who bought them." And man, weak, sinful man, must have something to do, or else his soul will soon get into an unhealthy state. We must have our hands filled, and our minds occupied with something, or else our imaginations will soon ferment and breed mischief.

And what is true of us, is true of our children too. Alas, indeed, for the man that has nothing to do! The Jews thought idleness a positive sin: it was a law of theirs that every man should bring up his son to some useful trade, — and they were right. They knew the heart of man better than some of us appear to do.

Idleness made Sodom what she was. "This was the iniquity of thy sister Sodom, pride, fulness of bread, and abundance of idleness was in her" (Ezek. 16:49). Idleness had much to do with David's awful sin with the wife of Uriah. — I see in 2 Sam. 11 that Joab went out to war against Ammon, "but David tarried still at Jerusalem." Was not that idle? And then it was that he saw Bathsheba, — and the next step we read of is his tremendous and miserable fall.

Verily, I believe that idleness has led to more sin than almost any other habit that could be named. I suspect it is the mother of many a work of the flesh,

— the mother of adultery, fornication, drunkenness, and many other deeds of darkness that I have not time to name. Let your own conscience say whether I do not speak the truth. You were idle, and at once the devil knocked at the door and came in.

And indeed I do not wonder; — everything in the world around us seems to teach the same lesson. It is the still water which becomes stagnant and impure: the running, moving streams are always clear. If you have steam machinery, you must work it, or it soon gets out of order. If you have a horse, you must exercise him; he is never so well as when he has regular work. If you would have good bodily health yourself, you must take exercise. If you always sit still, your body is sure at length to complain. And just so is it with the soul. The active moving mind is a hard mark for the devil to shoot at. Try to be always full of useful employment, and thus your enemy will find it difficult to get room to sow tares. Reader, I ask you to set these things before the minds of your children. Teach them the value of time, and try to make them learn the habit of using it well. It pains me to see children idling over what they have in hand, whatever it may be. I love to see them active and industrious, and giving their whole heart to all they do; giving their whole heart to lessons, when they have to learn;

— giving their whole heart even to their amusements, when they go to play.

But if you love them well, let idleness be counted a sin in your family.

12
FEAR OVER-INDULGENCE

Train them with a constant fear of over-indulgence.

This is the one point of all on which you have most need to be on your guard. It is natural to be tender and affectionate towards your own flesh and blood, and it is the excess of this very tenderness and affection which you have to fear. Take heed that it does not make you blind to your children's faults, and deaf to all advice about them. Take heed lest it make you overlook bad conduct, rather than have the pain of inflicting punishment and correction.

I know well that punishment and correction are disagreeable things. Nothing is more unpleasant than giving pain to those we love, and calling forth their tears. But so long as hearts are what hearts are, it is vain to suppose, as a general rule, that children can ever be brought up without correction.

Spoiling is a very expressive word, and sadly full of meaning. Now it is the shortest way to spoil children to let them have their own way, — to allow them to do wrong and not to punish them for it. Believe me, you must not do it, whatever pain it may cost you unless you wish to ruin your children's souls.

You cannot say that Scripture does not speak expressly on this subject: "He that spareth his rod, hateth his son; but he that loveth him, chasteneth him betimes" (Prov. 13:24). "Chasten thy son while there is hope, and let not thy soul spare for his crying" (Prov. 19:18). "Foolishness is bound in the heart of a child: but the rod of correction shall drive it from him" (Prov. 22:15). "Withhold not correction from the child, for if thou beatest him with the rod he shall not die. Thou shalt beat him with the rod, and deliver his soul from hell" (Prov. 23:13,14). "The rod and reproof give wisdom: but a child left to himself bringeth his mother to shame." "Correct thy son, and he shall give thee rest, yea, he shall give delight to thy soul" (Prov. 29:15,17).

How strong and forcible are these texts! How melancholy is the fact, that in many Christian families they seem almost unknown! Their children need reproof, but it is hardly ever given; they need correction, but it is hardly ever employed. And yet this book of Proverbs is not obsolete and unfit for Christians. It is given by inspiration of God, and profitable. It is given for our learning, even as the Epistles to the Romans and Ephesians. Surely the believer who brings up his children without attention to its counsel is making himself wise above that which is written, and greatly errs.

Fathers and mothers, I tell you plainly, if you never punish your children when they are in fault, you are doing them a grievous wrong. I warn you, this is the rock on which the saints of God, in every age, have only too frequently made shipwreck. I would fain persuade you to be wise in time, and keep clear of it. See it in Eli's case. His sons Hophni and Phinehas "made themselves vile, and he restrained them not." He gave them no more than a tame and lukewarm reproof, when he ought to have rebuked them sharply. In one word, he honoured his sons above God. And what was the end of these things? He lived to hear of the death of both his sons in battle, and his own grey hairs were brought down with sorrow to the grave (1 Sam. 2:22-29, 3:13).

See, too, the case of David. Who can read without pain the history of his children, and their sins? Amnon's incest, — Absalom's murder and proud rebellion, — Adonijah's scheming ambition: truly these were grievous wounds for the man after God's own heart to receive from his own house. But was there no fault on his side? I fear there can be no doubt there was. I find a clue to it all in the account of Adonijah in 1 Kings 1:6: "His father had not displeased him at any time in saying, Why hast thou done so?" There was the foundation of all the mischief. David was an over-indulgent father, — a father who let his children have their own way, — and he reaped according as he had sown.

Parents, I beseech you, for your children's sake, beware of over-indulgence. I call on you to remember, it is your first duty to consult their real interests, and not their fancies and likings; — to train them, not to humour them — to profit, not merely to please.

You must not give way to every wish and caprice of your child's mind, however much you may love him. You must not let him suppose his will is to be everything, and that he has only to desire a thing and it will be done. Do not, I pray you, make your children idols, lest God should take them away, and break your idol, just to convince you of your folly.

Learn to say "No" to your children. Show them that you are able to refuse whatever you think is not fit for them. Show them that you are ready to punish disobedience, and that when you speak of punishment, you are not only ready to threaten, but also to perform. Do not threaten too much[1]. Threatened folks, and threatened faults, live long. Punish seldom, but really and in good earnest, — frequent and slight punishment is a wretched system indeed[2].

Beware of letting small faults pass unnoticed under the idea "it is a little one." There are no little things in training children; all are important. Little weeds need plucking up as much as any. Leave them alone, and they will soon be great. Reader, if there be any point which deserves your attention, believe me, it is this one. It is one that will give you trouble, I know. But if you do not take trouble with your children when they are young, they will give you trouble when they are old. Choose which you prefer.

---

1. Some parents and nurses have a way of saying, "Naughty child," to a boy or girl on every slight occasion, and often without good cause. It is a very foolish habit. Words of blame should never be used without real reason.
2. As to the best way of punishing a child, no general rule can be laid down. The characters of children are so exceedingly different, that what would be a severe punishment to one child, would be no punishment at all to another. I only beg to enter my decided protest against the modern notion that no child ought ever to be whipped. Doubtless some parents use bodily correction far too much, and far too violently; but many others, I fear, use it far too little.

13
HOW GOD TRAINS HIS CHILDREN

Train them remembering continually how God trains His children.

The Bible tells us that God has an elect people, — a family in this world. All poor sinners who have been convinced of sin, and fled to Jesus for peace, make up that family. All of us who really believe on Christ for salvation are its members. Now God the Father is ever training the members of this family for their everlasting abode with Him in heaven. He acts as a husbandman pruning his vines, that they may bear more fruit. He knows the character of each of us, — our besetting sins, — our weaknesses, — our peculiar infirmities, — our special wants. He knows our works and where we dwell, who are our companions in life, and what are our trials, what our temptations, and what are our privileges. He knows all these things, and is ever ordering all for our good. He allots to each of us, in His providence, the very things we need, in order to bear the most fruit, — as much of sunshine as we can stand, and as much of rain, — as much of bitter things as we can bear, and as much of sweet. Reader, if you would train your children wisely, mark well how God the Father trains His. He doeth all things well; the plan which He adopts must be right.

See, then, how many things there are which God withholds from His children. Few could be found, I suspect, among them who have not had desires which He has never been pleased to fulfil. There has often been some one thing they wanted to attain, and yet there has always been some barrier to prevent attainment. It has been just as if God was placing it above our reach, and saying, "This is not good for you; this must not be." Moses desired exceedingly to cross over Jordan, and see the goodly land of promise; but you will remember his desire was never granted.

See, too, how often God leads His people by ways which seem dark and mysterious to our eyes. We cannot see the meaning of all His dealings with us; we cannot see the reasonableness of the path in which our feet are treading. Sometimes so many trials have assailed us, — so many difficulties encompassed us,

— that we have not been able to discover the needs-be of it all. It has been just as if our Father was taking us by the hand into a dark place and saying, "Ask no questions, but follow Me." There was a direct road from Egypt to Canaan, yet Israel was not led into it; but round, through the wilderness. And this seemed hard at the time. "The soul of the people," we are told, "was much discouraged because of the way" (Exod. 13:17; Num. 21:4).

See, also, how often God chastens His people with trial and affliction. He sends them crosses and disappointments; He lays them low with sickness; He strips them of property and friends; He changes them from one position to another; He visits them with things most hard to flesh and blood; and some of us have well- nigh fainted under the burdens laid upon us. We have felt pressed beyond strength, and have been almost ready to murmur at the hand which chastened us. Paul the Apostle had a thorn in the flesh appointed him, some bitter bodily trial, no doubt, though we know not exactly what it was. But this we know, — he besought the Lord thrice that it might be removed; yet it was not taken away (2 Cor. 12:8,9).

Now, reader, notwithstanding all these things, did you ever hear of a single child of God who thought his Father did not treat him wisely? No, I am sure you never did. God's children would always tell you, in the long run, it was a blessed thing they did not have their own way, and that God had done far better for them than they could have done for themselves. Yes! And they could tell you, too, that God's dealings had provided more happiness for them than they ever would have obtained themselves, and that His way, however dark at times, was the way of pleasantness and the path of peace.

I ask you to lay to heart the lesson which God's dealings with His people is meant to teach you. Fear not to withhold from your child anything you think will do him harm, whatever his own wishes may be. This is God's plan. Hesitate not to lay on him commands, of which he may not at present see the wisdom, and to guide him in ways which may not now seem reasonable to his mind. This is God's plan.

Shrink not from chastising and correcting him whenever you see his soul's health requires it, however painful it may be to your feelings; and remember medicines for the mind must not be rejected because they are bitter. This is God's plan.

And be not afraid, above all, that such a plan of training will make your child unhappy. I warn you against this delusion. Depend on it, there is no surer road to unhappiness than always having our own way. To have our wills checked and denied is a blessed thing for us; it makes us value enjoyments when they come. To be indulged perpetually is the way to be made selfish; and selfish people and spoiled children, believe me, are seldom happy.

Reader, be not wiser than God; — train your children as He trains His.

14
THE INFLUENCE OF YOUR EXAMPLE

Train them remembering continually the influence; of your own example.

Instruction, and advice, and commands will profit little, unless they are backed up by the pattern of your own life. Your children will never believe you are in earnest, and really wish them to obey you, so long as your actions contradict your counsel. Archbishop Tillotson made a wise remark when he said, "To give children good instruction, and a bad example, is but beckoning to them with the head to show them the way to heaven, while we take them by the hand and lead them in the way to hell."

We little know the force and power of example. No one of us can live to himself in this world; we are always influencing those around us, in one way or another, either for good or for evil, either for God or for sin. — They see our ways, they mark our conduct, they observe our behaviour, and what they see us practise, that they may fairly suppose we think right. And never, I believe, does example tell so powerfully as it does in the case of parents and children.

Fathers and mothers, do not forget that children learn more by the eye than they do by the ear. No school will make such deep marks on character as home. The best of schoolmasters will not imprint on their minds as much as they will pick up at your fireside. Imitation is a far stronger principle with children than memory. What they see has a much stronger effect on their minds than what they are told.

Take care, then, what you do before a child. It is a true proverb, "Who sins before a child, sins double." Strive rather to be a living epistle of Christ, such as your families can read, and that plainly too. Be an example of reverence for the Word of God, reverence in prayer, reverence for means of grace, reverence for the Lord's day. — Be an example in words, in temper, in diligence, in temperance, in faith, in charity, in kindness, in humility. Think not your children will practise what they do not see you do. You are their model picture, and they will copy what you are. Your reasoning and your lecturing, your wise commands and your good advice; all this they may not understand, but they can understand your life.

Children are very quick observers; very quick in seeing through some kinds of hypocrisy, very quick in finding out what you really think and feel, very quick in adopting all your ways and opinions. You will often find as the father is, so is the son.

Remember the word that the conqueror Caesar always used to his soldiers in a battle. He did not say "Go forward," but "Come." So it must be with you in training your children. They will seldom learn habits which they see you despise, or walk in paths in which you do not walk yourself. He that preaches to his children what he does not practise, is working a work that never goes forward. It is like the fabled web of Penelope of old, who wove all day, and unwove all night. Even so, the parent who tries to train without setting a good example is building with one hand, and pulling down with the other.

15
THE POWER OF SIN

Train them. remembering continually the power of sin.

I name this shortly, in order to guard you against unscriptural expectations. You must not expect to find your children's minds a sheet of pure white paper, and to have no trouble if you only use right means. I warn you plainly you will find no such thing. It is painful to see how much corruption and evil there is in a young child's heart, and how soon it begins to bear fruit. Violent tempers, self- will, pride, envy, sullenness, passion, idleness, selfishness, deceit, cunning, falsehood, hypocrisy, a terrible aptness to learn what is bad, a painful slowness to learn what is good, a readiness to pretend anything in order to gain their own ends, — all these things, or some of them, you must be prepared to see, even in your own flesh and blood. In little ways they will creep out at a very early age; it is almost startling to observe how naturally they seem to spring up. Children require no schooling to learn to sin.

But you must not be discouraged and cast down by what you see. You must not think it a strange and unusual thing, that little hearts can be so full of sin. It is the only portion which our father Adam left us; it is that fallen nature with which we come into the world; it is that inheritance which belongs to us all. Let it rather make you more diligent in using every means which seem most likely, by God's blessing, to counteract the mischief. Let it make you more and more careful, so far as in you lies, to keep your children out of the way of temptation.

Never listen to those who tell you your children are good, and well brought up, and can be trusted. Think rather that their hearts are always inflammable as tinder. At their very best, they only want a spark to set their corruptions alight. Parents are seldom too cautious. Remember the natural depravity of your children, and take care.

16
THE PROMISES OF SCRIPTURE

Train them remembering continually the promises of Scripture.

I name this also shortly, in order to guard you against discouragement. You have a plain promise on your side, "Train up your child in the way he should go, and when he is old he shall not depart from it" (Prov. 22:6). Think what it is to have a promise like this. Promises were the only lamp of hope which cheered the hearts of the patriarchs before the Bible was written. Enoch, Noah, Abrahanm, Isaac, Jacob, Joseph, — all lived on a few promises, and prospered in their souls. Promises are the cordials which in every age have supported and strengthened the believer. He that has got a plain text upon his side need never be cast down. Fathers and mothers, when your hearts are failing, and ready to halt, look at the word of this text, and take comfort.

Think who it is that promises. It is not the word of a man, who may lie or repent; it is the word of the King of kings, who never changes. Hath He said a thing, and shall He not do it? Or hath He spoken, and shall He not make it good? Neither is anything too hard for Him to perform. The things that are impossible with men are possible with God. Reader, if we get not the benefit of the promise we are dwelling upon, the fault is not in Him, but in ourselves.

Think, too, what the promise contains, before you refuse to take comfort from it. It speaks of a certain time when good training shall especially bear fruit, — "when a child is old." Surely there is comfort in this. You may not see with your own eyes the result of careful training, but you know not what blessed fruits may not spring from it, long after you are dead and gone. It is not God's way to give everything at once. "Afterwards' is the time when He often chooses to work, both in the things of nature and in the things of grace. "Afterward" is the season when affliction bears the peaceable fruit of righteousness (Heb. 12:11). "Afterward" was the time when the son who refused to work in his father's vineyard repented and went (Matt. 21:29). And "afterward" is the time to which parents must look forward if they see not success at once, — you must sow in hope and plant in hope.

Cast thy bread upon the waters," saith the Spirit, "for thou shalt find it after many days" (Eceles. 11:1). Many children, I doubt not, shall rise up in the day of judgment, and bless their parents for good training, who never gave any signs of having profited by it during their parents' lives. Go forward then in faith, and be sure that your labour shall not be altogether thrown away. Three times did Elijah stretch himself upon the widow's child before it revived. Take example from him, and persevere.

17
CONTINUAL PRAYER FOR BLESSING

Train them, lastly, with continual prayer for a blessing on all you do.

Without the blessing of the Lord, your best endeavours will do no good. He has the hearts of all men in His hands, and except He touch the hearts of your children by His Spirit, you will weary yourself to no purpose. Water, therefore, the seed you sow on their minds with unceasing prayer. The Lord is far more willing to hear than we to pray; far more ready to give blessings than we to ask them ; — but He loves to be entreated for them. And I set this matter of prayer before you, as the top-stone and seal of all you do. I suspect the child of many prayers is seldom cast away.

Look upon your children as Jacob did on his; he tells Esau they are "the children which God hath graciously given thy servant" (Gen. 33:5). Look on them as Joseph did on his; he told his father, "They are the sons whom God hath given me" (Gen. 48:9). Count them with the Psalmist to be "an heritage and reward from the Lord" (Ps. 127:3). And then ask the Lord, with a holy boldness, to be gracious and merciful to His own gifts. Mark how Abraham intercedes for Ishmael, because he loved him, "Oh that Ishmael might live before thee" (Gen. 17:18). See how Manoah speaks to the angel about Samson, "How shall we order the child, and how shall we do unto him?" (Judg. 13:12). Observe how tenderly Job cared for his children's souls, "He offered burnt-offerings according to the number of them all, for he said, It may be my sons have sinned, and cursed God in their hearts. Thus did Job continually" (Job 1:5). Parents, if you love your children, go and do likewise. You cannot name their names before the mercy-seat too often.

And now, reader, in conclusion, let me once more press upon you the necessity and importance of using every single means in your power, if you would train children for heaven.

I know well that God is a sovereign God, and

doeth all things according to the counsel of His own will. I know that Rehoboam was the son of Solomon, and Manasseh the son of Hezekiah, and that you do not always see godly parents having a godly seed. But I know also that God is a God who works by means, and sure am I, if you make light of such means as I have mentioned, your children are not likely to turn out well.

Fathers and mothers, you may take your children to be baptized, and have them enrolled in the ranks of Christ's Church; — you may get godly sponsors to answer for them, and help you by their prayers; — you may send them to the best of schools, and give them Bibles and Prayer Books, and fill them with head knowledge but if all this time there is no regular training at home, I tell you plainly, I fear it will go hard in the end with your children's souls. Home is the place where habits are formed; — home is the place where the foundations of character are laid; — home gives the bias to our tastes, and likings, and opinions. See then, I pray you, that there be careful training at home. Happy indeed is the man who can say, as Bolton did upon his dying bed, to his children, "I do believe not one of you will dare to meet me before the tribunal of Christ in an unregenerate state."

Fathers and mothers, I charge you solemnly

before God and the Lord Jesus Christ, take every pains to train your children in the way they should go. I charge you not merely for the sake of your children's souls; I charge you for the sake of your own future comfort and peace. Truly it is your interest so to do. Truly your own happiness in great measure depends on it. Children have ever been the bow from which the sharpest arrows have pierced man's heart.

Children have mixed the bitterest cups that man has ever had to drink. Children have caused the saddest tears that man has ever had to shed. Adam could tell you so; Jacob could tell you so; David could tell you so. There are no sorrows on earth like those which children have brought upon their parents. Oh! take heed, lest your own neglect should lay up misery for you in your old age. Take heed, lest you weep under the ill-treatment of a thankless child, in the days when your eye is dim, and your natural force abated.

If ever you wish your children to be the restorers of your life, and the nourishers of your old age, — if you would have them blessings and not curses — joys and not sorrows — Judahs and not Reubens — Ruths and not Orpahs, — if you would not, like Noah, be ashamed of their deeds, and, like Rebekah, be made weary of your life by them: if this be your wish, remember my advice betimes, train them while young in the right way.

And as for me, I will conclude by putting up my prayer to God for all who read this paper, that you may all be taught of God to feel the value of your own souls. This is one reason why baptism is too often a mere form, and Christian training despised and disregarded. Too often parents feel not for themselves, and so they feel not for their children. They do not realize the tremendous difference between a state of nature and a state of grace, and therefore they are content to let them alone.

Now the Lord teach you all that sin is that abominable thing which God hateth. Then, I know you will mourn over the sins of your children, and strive to pluck them out as brands from the fire.

The Lord teach you all how precious Christ is, and what a mighty and complete work He hath done for our salvation. Then, I feel confident you will use every means to bring your children to Jesus, that they may live through Him. The Lord teach you all your need of the Holy Spirit, to renew, sanctify, and quicken your souls. Then, I feel sure you will urge your children to pray for Him without ceasing, and never rest till He has come down into their hearts with power, and made them new creatures.

The Lord grant this, and then I have a good hope that you will indeed train up your children well, — train well for this life, and train well for the life to come; train well for earth, and train well for heaven; train them for God, for Christ, and for eternity.

Copyright © 2020 by FV Éditions
Ebook ISBN : 979-10-299-1014-2
Paperback ISBN : 979-10-299-1015-9
Hardcover ISBN : 979-10-299-1016-6
All rights reserved.

www.ingramcontent.com/pod-product-compliance
Lightning Source LLC
LaVergne TN
LVHW092058060526
838201LV00047B/1446